AIR FRYER DESSERT RECIPES

By Sarah Flores

Copyright © 2017 by Sarah Flores

All Rights Reserved. This document is geared towards providing exact and reliable information in regards to the topic and issue covered. The publication is sold with the idea that the publisher is not required to render accounting, officially permitted, or otherwise, qualified services. If advice is necessary, legal or professional, a practiced individual in the profession should be ordered.

- From a Declaration of Principles which was accepted and approved equally by a Committee of the American Bar Association and a Committee of Publishers and Associations.

In no way is it legal to reproduce, duplicate, or transmit any part of this document in either electronic means or in printed format. Recording of this publication is strictly prohibited and any storage of this document is not allowed unless with written permission from the publisher. All rights reserved.

The information provided herein is stated to be truthful and consistent, in that any liability, in terms of inattention or otherwise, by any usage or abuse of any policies, processes, or directions contained within is the solitary and utter responsibility of the recipient reader. Under no circumstances will any legal responsibility or blame be held against the publisher for any reparation, damages, or monetary loss due to the information herein, either directly or indirectly.

Respective authors own all copyrights not held by the publisher.

The information herein is offered for informational purposes solely, and is universal as so. The presentation of the information is without contract or any type of guarantee assurance.

The trademarks that are used are without any consent, and the publication of the trademark is without permission or backing by the trademark owner. All trademarks and brands within this book are for clarifying purposes only and are the owned by the owners themselves, not affiliated with this document.

Disclaimer and Terms of Use: The Author and Publisher has strived to be as accurate and complete as possible in the creation of this book, notwithstanding the fact that he does not warrant or represent at any time that the contents within are accurate due to the rapidly changing nature of the Internet. While all attempts have been made to verify information provided in this publication, the Author and Publisher assumes no responsibility for errors, omissions, or contrary interpretation of the subject matter herein.

Any perceived slights of specific persons, peoples, or organizations are unintentional. In practical advice books, like anything else in life, there are no guarantees of results. Readers are cautioned to rely on their own judgment about their individual circumstances and act accordingly.

This book is not intended for use as a source of legal, medical, business, accounting or financial advice. All readers are advised to seek services of competent professionals in the legal, medical, business, accounting, and finance fields.

TABLE OF CONTENTS

AIRFRYER DESSERTS 7
   Tropical meringue 8
   Ricotta and lemon cheesecake 10
   Tarte Tatin 11
   Stuffed Baked Apples 13
   Mother's Day cake 15
   Red berry Pavlova 17
   Raspberry yogurt ice cream 19
   Pineapple with Honey and Coconut 21
   Chocolate cake 22
   Lemon meringue pie 24
   Cranberry Muffins 27
   Crème brûlée 29
   Brownies 31
   Cherry Clafoutis 33
   Apple crisp cookie cake 35
   Apple pie 37
   Apricot and Blackberry Crumble 39
   Apples Stuffed with Almonds 41
   Blueberry muffins 42
   Pear parcel 43

Fruit Crumble Mug Cakes 44
Airfryer Chocolate Mug Cake 46
British Lemon Tarts 47
White Chocolate Chip Cookies 49
Pineapple Cake 50
Banana Bread 52
Airfryer Doughnuts 53
Airfryer Chocolate Eclairs 55
Airfryer Chocolate Brownies 57
Mini Apple Pies 59
Heart Shaped Cookies 60
Chocolate Christmas Biscuits 61
Airfryer Oaty Sandwich Biscuits 63
Airfryer Lemon Biscuits 65
Half Dipped Chocolate Biscuits 66

VEGAN DESSERTS 67

Coffee Doughnut Holes 68
Vegan Air Fryer Blueberry Apple Crumble 70
Chili-Ginger Tahini Dressing 71
Salty Pistachio Brownies 72
Vegan Pumpkin Bread Pudding 74
Vegan Irish Cream Cheesecake 76
Cranberry-Carrot Cake 78
Vegan Gluten-Free Peach Cobbler 80
Pear Spice Upside-Down Cake 82
Banana Bread Pudding 85

Date-Sweetened Zucchini Brownies with Chocolate-Peanut Butter Frosting.. 87

Apple Pie Oatmeal Cookies 89

Pumpkin Oatmeal Cakes with Apple-Pecan Compote 91

Peach Oatmeal Bars..93

Applesauce Ginger Cake with Maple Glaze..95

AIRFRYER DESSERTS

TROPICAL MERINGUE

Serves: 4

Cook Time: 60 minutes

INGREDIENTS

- 5 eggs, separated
- 100 g super-fine sugar
- 2 teaspoons cornstarch, sieved
- 1 mango
- 4 passion fruit
- 1 papaya
- 1 pineapple
- 1 teaspoon lemon juice
- ½ tablespoon powdered sugar
- 200 ml whipped cream
- Parchment paper
- Chocolate to garnish

DIRECTIONS

1. Separate the eggs and then put the egg whites in a clean, grease-free bowl. Beat the egg white until fluffy with a mixer or in the food processor and gradually add the cornstarch and 80 g sugar. The egg whites are ready when they form peaks.

2. Take two sheets of parchment paper and cut to size for your Airfryer

grill pan. Spoon the egg white onto the two sheets of parchment paper. Dry these one by one in the Airfryer, for 60 minutes at 100 degrees. Remove and let the dried egg white cool for 5 minutes, then carefully remove from the parchment paper. Place the egg white upside down and let it dry.

3. Chop the papaya, mango and pineapple into very small cubes and keep 100 g of each in a separate container. This is the garnish. Puree the rest of the fruit, the contents of two passion fruits and lemon juice with your hand blender to produce a coulis.

4. Whip the cream with 20 g sugar until stiff and transfer to a piping bag with star nozzle. Place the remaining fruit on the meringue and drizzle with the coulis. Garnish the tropical meringue with whipped cream and powdered sugar.

RICOTTA AND LEMON CHEESECAKE

Serves: 4

Cook Time: 10 minutes

INGREDIENTS

- 1 (organic) lemon
- 500 g ricotta
- 150 g sugar
- 2 tsp vanilla essence
- 3 eggs
- 3 tbsp corn starch
- 20 cm round oven dish

DIRECTIONS

1. Preheat the Airfryer to 160°C.
2. Zest and juice the lemon. In a bowl, combine the ricotta, sugar, vanilla essence, 1 tbsp lemon juice and the lemon zest. Stir the ingredients until they are well combined and form a homogenous consistency.
3. Add the eggs one at a time and stir well. Add the corn starch and mix well. Pour the mixture into the oven dish.
4. Place the dish into the Airfryer basket and slide the basket into the Airfryer. Set the timer for 25 minutes. The cheesecake is ready when the timer rings and the centre is set. Place the dish on a wire rack and leave to cool completely.

TARTE TATIN

Serves: 4

Cook Time: 20 minutes

INGREDIENTS

- 60 g cold butter, in thin slices
- 1 egg yolk
- 100 g flour
- 1 large, firm apple (Elstar, Jonagold)
- 30 g sugar
- Small, round fixed-base cake pan, 15 cm diameter

DIRECTIONS

1. Cut 25 g of the butter slices into pieces and mix them into the flour with the egg yolk. Add a few drops of water, if necessary, and knead the mixture until it forms a smooth ball of dough.
2. On a floured work surface, roll out the dough to a 15 cm round.
3. Preheat the airfryer to 200°C.
4. Peel and core the apple and slice the fruit into 12 wedges.
5. Place the remaining butter slices in the pan and sprinkle the sugar over them. Place the apple wedges on top of this in a circular pattern.
6. Cover the apple wedges with the rolled-out dough and press the dough down along the inside edge of the cake pan.

7. Put the cake pan in the fryer basket and slide the basket into the airfryer. Set the timer to 25 minutes and bake until the tarte tatin is done. Immediately after baking, place a plate on the cake pan and flip the cake pan and the plate together so that the tart drops out onto the plate. Serve the tarte tatin hot or lukewarm in slices with ice cream or vanilla sauce.

STUFFED BAKED APPLES

Serves: 4

Cook Time: 20 minutes

INGREDIENTS

- 2 small apples
- 1 tablespoon raisins
- 2 sheets of ready-to-use puff pastry, 10 x 10 cm
- 2 tablespoons milk
- Pizza pan, 15 cm diameter

DIRECTIONS

1. Preheat the airfryer to 180°C.
2. Peel and core the apples. Enlarge the hollowed-out core a little by scooping out some extra apple.
3. Mix the raisins and the jam.
4. Place an apple on each slice of dough and fill the hollowed-out core with the raisin mixture. Fold the dough around the apple, enclosing it completely.
5. Place the stuffed apples on the pizza pan with the dough seams facing downward. Then brush the dough with milk.
6. Put the pizza pan in the fryer basket and slide the basket into the airfryer. Set the timer to 20 minutes and bake the stuffed apples until golden brown and done.

7. Allow the stuffed baked apples to cool until they are lukewarm and serve them with a scoop of ice cream or vanilla quark (curd cheese).

8. Variations: Fill the apples with: - Chopped dried apricots, cinnamon and ½ tablespoon soft brown sugar - Dried cranberries, 1 teaspoon scrapings of vanilla pod and ½ tablespoon sugar - Raisins, ½ tablespoon grated orange peel and ½ tablespoon brown sugar.

MOTHER'S DAY CAKE

Serves: 4

Cook Time: 10 minutes

INGREDIENTS

- For the sponge:
- 150 g sugar
- 150 g flour, sifted
- 5 eggs
- Pinch of salt
- Cream:
- 700 ml whole milk
- 1 vanilla pod
- 7 egg yolks
- 100 g powdered sugar
- 80 g cornstarch
- 1 teaspoon lemon juice
- 3 tablespoons strawberry jam
- Red food coloring
- Decoration:
- Red and white love heart candies
- 4 fresh strawberries

DIRECTIONS

1. First we make the sponge cake. This recipe is for a 22 cm tin. It's best to bake the dough without the basket or on the grill pan.

2. Put the sugar, eggs and salt in a bowl. Mix at the highest speed for 10 minutes. Spoon the flour little by little into the airy mixture. Grease the spring form, spoon in the mixture and bake at 155 degrees for 25 minutes. The sponge cake is ready when golden brown in color and it springs back after touching.

3. To make the yellow cream, slice open the first vanilla pod and scrape out the seeds. Put the milk in a pan and add the vanilla pod and seeds. Bring the milk slowly to the boil. Turn the heat down low and let the vanilla infuse the milk.

4. Meanwhile, whisk the egg yolks together with the sugar until creamy. Then carefully spoon in the corn starch. Remove the vanilla pod from the milk and remove the pan from the heat. Add a little of the hot milk to the egg mixture and stir well. Pour it in the remaining milk and bring to the boil, stirring. Let it cook gently for 5 minutes and keep stirring so the cream doesn't burn. Sieve the cream, leave to cool and set aside in the refrigerator. Tip: place a piece of plastic wrap over it to stop a yellow skin from forming.

RED BERRY PAVLOVA

Serves: 4

Cook Time: 10 minutes

INGREDIENTS

- 1 lemon, washed
- 5 eggs, separated
- 100 g super-fine sugar
- 2 teaspoons cornstarch, sieved
- 50 g strawberries
- 50 g raspberries
- 50 g black grapes
- 25 g blueberries
- 1 teaspoon lemon juice
- ½ tablespoon powdered sugar
- 200 ml whipped cream
- Red food coloring

DIRECTIONS

1. Heat the Airfryer to 160 degrees. Grate the zest of the lemon - only the skin, the pith is very bitter - and squeeze the fruit.

2. Beat the egg whites until stiff in a dry, clean bowl. Gradually add the super-fine sugar, corn starch, lemon juice and coloring. The egg whites are ready when they become shiny and form peaks.

3. Cut a piece of parchment paper to size and place on the grill pan accessory. Smooth the paper with the mixture to create a lovely pattern. Place the pan in the Airfryer, set the temperature to 100 degrees and bake for 45 minutes. We preheat the Airfryer at a higher temperature so that it is nice and hot when the meringue goes in, stopping it from running.

4. Switch off the Airfryer after the cooking time, but leave it shut. Leave the meringue in the warm Airfryer for 60 minutes. Then remove from the Airfryer and leave to cool.

5. Meanwhile, mix the fruit, keeping a little behind for garnish, and whip the cream until stiff. Once the meringue has cooled, carefully cut it horizontally through the center. Pipe or spread the whipped cream on the bottom layer and fill with the fruit. Place the other half on top and garnish with the rest of the fruit.

6. So nice that its almost a shame to eat. A lovely festive dessert!

RASPBERRY YOGURT ICE CREAM

Serves: 4

Cook Time: 10 minutes

INGREDIENTS

- 500 g raspberries (frozen)
- 2 tablespoons agave syrup
- 500 ml yogurt
- 125 g fresh raspberries
- 125 g fresh blueberries
- 3 sheets puff pastry
- 250 ml whipped cream
- 1 packet vanilla sugar

DIRECTIONS

1. Put half of the frozen raspberries, together with the cold yogurt and agave syrup in the SoupMaker. Select program 4. When this is done, just add the other half of the frozen raspberries and blend this together using program 5. Pour the ice cream into a container and leave for at least 2 hours in the freezer.

2. Whip the cream with the vanilla sugar and add half of the fresh raspberries and the entire container of blueberries. Put this in a piping bag. Meanwhile, make a coulis from the remaining raspberries by pureeing them with a hand blender.

3. Put the Extra-layer accessory in your Airfryer, grease with a small amount of oil and heat. Cut the pastry slices into three equal strips. Place three strips on the accessory and put the bottom of a spring form tin on top. Bake at 170 degrees for 15 minutes. Open the Airfryer during baking and carefully press (with a kitchen cloth or oven glove) down on the tin so that beautiful lines are created in the puff pastry while baking. Repeat with the other six strips of pastry. Leave the pastry to cool.

4. Pipe the whipped cream on the smooth side of a puff pastry slice and place the other side against it. Scoop out two balls of the raspberry ice cream and garnish with the coulis.

PINEAPPLE WITH HONEY AND COCONUT

Serves: 4

Cook Time: 10 minutes

INGREDIENTS

- ½ small fresh pineapple
- 1 tablespoon honey
- ½ tablespoon lime juice
- ¼ liter ice cream or mango sorbet
- Parchment paper

DIRECTIONS

1. Preheat the airfryer to 200°C. Line the bottom of the basket with baking parchment, leave 1 cm of the edge open.
2. Cut the pineapple lengthways into eight sections. Cut away the skin with the deep crowns and also remove the tough core.
3. Mix the honey with the lime juice in a bowl. Brush the pineapple sections with the honey and put them in the basket. Sprinkle the coconut on top.
4. Slide the basket into the airfryer and set the timer to 12 minutes. The pineapple with the coconut should be hot and golden brown.
5. Serve the pineapple sections on plates, each with a generous scoop of ice cream next to it.

CHOCOLATE CAKE

Serves: 4

Cook Time: 30 minutes

INGREDIENTS

- 3 eggs
- 125 ml sour cream
- 150 g flour
- 150 g caster sugar
- 125 g unsalted butter
- 40 g cocoa powder
- 1 tsp baking powder
- ½ tsp bicarbonate of soda
- 2 tsp vanilla essence
- Chocolate icing:
- 150 g chocolate
- 50 g unsalted softened butter
- 200 g icing sugar
- 1 tsp vanilla essence

DIRECTIONS

1. Preheat the Airfryer to 160°C.

2. Place all the cake ingredients into a food processor and mix well. Transfer to the oven dish.

3. Place the oven dish into the basket of the Airfryer. Slide the basket into the Airfryer and set the timer for 25 minutes. Once the time is up and the timer rings, prick the cake with a wooden skewer or fork. If it comes out clean, the cake is cooked through. If it's still sticky, place the cake back into the Airfryer and set the timer for another 5minutes.

4. Remove the dish from the basket and leave the cake to cool on a wire rack.

5. Meanwhile, melt the chocolate au bain marie or in the microwave. Leave to cool a little, then mix all of the icing ingredients together.

6. Remove the cooled cake from the oven dish and place it onto a plate. Cover with the chocolate icing and serve.

LEMON MERINGUE PIE

Serves: 4

Cook Time: 20 minutes

INGREDIENTS

- For the dough:
- 30 g powdered sugar
- 65 g sugar
- 30 g ground almonds
- 250 g flour
- 125 g butter (room temperature)
- 1 egg
- 1 pinch of salt
- 1 vanilla pod
- For the filling:
- 100 ml lemon juice
- Grated peel of 2 lemons
- 300 g powdered sugar
- 300 g butter
- 3 egg yolks
- 2 eggs
- For the meringue:
- 200 ml egg whites (approximately 8)
- Vinegar

- 200 g sugar
- 160 g powdered sugar
- For decoration:
- Cape gooseberry
- Lemon
- Spun sugar
- Yellow food coloring

DIRECTIONS

1. Weigh out the ingredients for the dough. Mix the butter with the sugar and the ground almonds. Cut the vanilla pod in two halves and use a knife to scrape out the seeds. Mix the vanilla with the egg, salt, flour and sugar until homogeneous. If you have a food processor, you can let it do the work. Wrap the dough in plastic wrap and leave in the refrigerator for an hour.

2. Now for the lemon cream. Melt the butter at a moderate heat and add the lemon juice and zest. Then add the powdered sugar, stir well and briefly bring to the boil. Beat the eggs and egg yolks. Remove the pan from the heat and mix the eggs together with the butter, sugar and lemon until smooth. Place the pan on the heat and keep stirring, so that the egg does not solidify. Pass the mixture through a fine sieve into a bowl. Cover the bowl with plastic wrap and leave for at least one hour in the refrigerator. If youvve made more cream than in the recipe, for example, double the amount, it will need longer to set.

3. For the meringue, weigh out all the ingredients. Put a few drops of vinegar on a paper towel and degrease the mixing bowl. Put the egg whites in the bowl and whip until stiff while you slowly add the sugar. Sift the powdered sugar into the beaten egg whites and beat a little more. Put the egg whites in a piping bag.

4. Remove the dough from the refrigerator and roll it out to about half a centimeter thick. Take a loose bottomed cake tin that fits in your Airfryer and grease. Place the dough in the tin, press down well and

prick some holes. If you have baking beans you can use these, putting a sheet of parchment paper on the dough then the beans on top. Heat the Airfryer to 160 and bake the casing for 30 minutes.

5. For the meringue, weigh out all the ingredients. Put a few drops of vinegar on a paper towel and degrease the mixing bowl. Put the egg whites in the bowl and whip until stiff while you slowly add the sugar. Sift the powdered sugar into the beaten egg whites and beat a little more. Put the egg whites in a piping bag.

CRANBERRY MUFFINS

Serves: 4

Cook Time: 10 minutes

INGREDIENTS

- 75 g flour
- 1½ teaspoons baking powder
- 1 teaspoon cinnamon
- 3 tablespoons sugar
- 1 small egg
- 75 ml milk
- 50 g butter, melted
- 75 g dried cranberries
- 8 paper muffin cups

DIRECTIONS

1. Preheat the airfryer to 200°C. Double up the muffin cups to form four cups in total.
2. Sift the flour into a bowl and add the baking powder, cinnamon, sugar and a pinch of salt. Mix well.
3. In another bowl, lightly beat the egg and add the milk and melted butter. Mix well. Stir this mixture into the flour. Then add the cranberries and mix.
4. Spoon the batter into the doubled muffin cups and carefully place them in the fryer basket.

5. Slide the basket into the airfryer and set the timer to 15 minutes. Bake the muffins until they are golden brown and done. Let the muffins cool in the cups.

6. Variations: Replace the cranberries with: - 75 g blueberries - 75 g chopped apple mixed with 1 tablespoon lemon juice - 75 g chopped dates with 1 tablespoon orange juice - 100 g pure chocolate (70% cocoa) with 1 tablespoon grated orange peel

7. Savory Muffins: Replace sugar and cinnamon with 50 g grated cheese and add one of the following to the batter: - 75 g boiled ham in strips with 2 tablespoons finely chopped parsley - 75 g coarsely chopped and roasted hazelnuts, pistachios or pecans

CRÈME BRÛLÉE

Serves: 4

Cook Time: 10 minutes

INGREDIENTS

- 2 vanilla pods
- 250 ml whipped cream
- 250 ml milk
- 10 eggs
- 100 g sugar
- 70 g super-fine sugar
- Garnish:
- 2 tablespoons brown sugar candy
- 2 tablespoons super-fine white sugar
- Blueberries
- Redcurrants
- Spun sugar (if desired)

DIRECTIONS

1. Pour the cream and milk in a pan. Cut open the vanilla pods and scrape the seeds out. Add to the cream and milk. Also add the vanilla pods, because they still give flavor. Heat the mixture on a medium heat (almost to boiling) and stir regularly with a whisk.

2. Take two bowls. Break the eggs and separate the egg yolks from the egg whites. You don›t need the whites. Beat the yolks with a whisk and

add the granulated sugar and white super-fine sugar. Mix carefully, but don›t make it too frothy. Remove the vanilla pods from the milk and cream and pour the warm mixture into the beaten yolks, constantly stirring. Let the mixture rest for approximately 20 to 30 minutes.

3. Fill the oven dishes with the mixture. Cook the crème brûlées for 50 minutes at 90 degrees. You can test how it's set by shaking the dish gently. Let them cool fully.

4. Mix the granulated sugar and brown sugar candy in the blender or mincer. You now have the ideal sugar mixture for the crunchy layer. Sprinkle a fine layer of sugar on each dish and caramelize the sugar using a small kitchen blowtorch. The sugar should melt and caramelize, but must not burn.

5. Garnish the crème brûlées with the berries and, if you like, some spun sugar.

BROWNIES

Serves: 4

Cook Time: 30 minutes

INGREDIENTS

- 200g butter
- 100g dark chocolate
- 100g white chocolate
- 4 small eggs
- 200g sugar
- 2 tablespoons of vanilla extract
- 100g flour
- 150g pecan nuts, chopped
- 1 cake tin 20 x 20 cm, greased

DIRECTIONS

1. Preheat the oven to 180 oC. Melt half of the butter with the dark chocolate in a thick-bottomed pan, and melt the white chocolate in another pan with the rest of the butter. Leave to cool.

2. Using the mixer, beat the eggs briefly with the sugar and vanilla. Divide the flour into 2 portions and add a pinch of salt to each.

3. Beat half of the egg-sugar mixture through the dark chocolate. Then add in half of the flour and half of the nuts and mix. Do the same with the white chocolate mixture.

4. Pour the white and brown brownie mixture into two different sides of the cake tin. Use a spatula to partially mix the two colours, creating a swirl. Bake the brownies for about 30 minutes. When ready, the surface should be dry to touch.

CHERRY CLAFOUTIS

Serves: 4

Cook Time: 20 minutes

INGREDIENTS

- 200 g fresh cherries or 1 jar of cherries, well-drained
- 2-3 tablespoons crème de cassis or vodka
- 50 g flour
- 2 tablespoons sugar
- 1 egg
- 125 ml sour cream
- 10 g butter
- Powdered sugar
- Small, low cake pan, 15 cm diameter

DIRECTIONS

1. Pit the cherries and mix them in a bowl with the kirsch or crème de cassis.
2. Preheat the airfryer to 180°C.
3. In another bowl, mix the flour with the sugar, a pinch of salt, the egg and the sour cream until the dough is smooth and thick. Add a drop or two of water, if necessary.
4. Spoon the batter into the buttered cake pan. Place the cherries evenly over the top of the batter and place the remaining butter in small chunks evenly on top.

5. Put the cake pan in the fryer basket and slide the basket into the airfryer. Set the timer to 25 minutes. Bake the clafoutis until it is golden brown and done.

6. Immediately after baking, dust the clafoutis with plenty of powdered sugar. Serve the clafoutis lukewarm in slices.

APPLE CRISP COOKIE CAKE

Serves: 4

Cook Time: 10 minutes

INGREDIENTS

- For the sponge:
- 5 egg whites
- 125 g sugar
- 125 g self-rising flour
- For the apple crisp:
- 100 g oats
- 125 g flour
- 115 g chilled butter
- 100 g sugar
- 1 pinch of ground cinnamon
- 1 pinch of ground cardamom
- 1 pinch of ground star anise
- 4 cooking apples
- 4 tablespoons brown sugar
- For the topping:
- 1 packet mini butter wafer cookies
- 500 ml whipped cream
- 100 g sugar

DIRECTIONS

1. To make the sponge, whisk the sugar and the egg whites together in the food processor (on the highest setting) until light and airy. You know its ready when it turns completely white and your whisk leaves a mark.

2. Sieve the flour and spoon this carefully through the whisked egg whites. Transfer the batter into a greased cake tin and bake at 150 degrees for 30 minutes until cooked. You can see whether the sponge is done by gently pressing on it. If it springs back, the cake is cooked. Place a cloth on the worktop, sprinkle a little sugar on to prevent sticking and leave the dough to cool.

3. To make the crisp, weigh out all of the ingredients and cut your cold butter into cubes. Mix the following ingredients in a large bowl; flour, apple, oats, sugar and butter cubes. Season the mixture with the ground cinnamon, ground star anise and the cardamom. Knead all the ingredients into a breadcrumb-like dough.

4. Preheat the oven to 200 degrees. Peel the apples and cut them into small pieces. Take an oven dish and fill with the pieces of apple. Sprinkle the brown sugar over the apples and mix well. Spread the crisp dough over the oven dish. Bake 25 to 30 minutes and leave to cool. You can also prepare the crisp in the Airfryer using the baking accessory. The cooking time is 20 minutes at 170 degrees.

5. Cut the sponge into three equal slices. Beat the cream with the sugar in the food processor until stiff. Now build up the cake as follows: put the apple crisp on top of the first sponge layer. Add the cream on top. Repeat this step twice. Top the cake with cream and apple. Place the little cookies in the cream.

APPLE PIE

Serves: 4

Cook Time: 10 minutes

INGREDIENTS

- For the dough:
- 125 g butter or margarine
- 125 g superfine sugar
- 250 g self-rising flour
- Salt
- ½ lemon
- For the filling:
- 1.5 kg tart apples
- 60 g golden raisins
- 10 g currants
- 2 tablespoons vanilla custard
- 5 tablespoons apricot jam
- 200 g sugar
- Pinch of cinnamon
- For decoration:
- Powdered sugar

DIRECTIONS

1. Clean the lemon, grate the peel and squeeze the fruit. Mix the butter with the sugar, the lemon juice, the lemon peel and a pinch of salt until combined. Then rub the self-rising flour into the butter mixture.

2. Peel and slice the apples. Mix with the raisins, currants, custard, apricot jam, cinnamon and sugar.

3. Roll the dough out to 28 cm (for one tin in the Airfryer Avance XL) or divide into three and roll out to 20 cm each (for three tins in the Airfryer Viva). Grease the tin(s) with a little melted butter and place a sheet of parchment paper on it/them. Put the dough in the tin and press down level. To avoid air bubbles, prick holes in the base with a fork. Spread the filling on top and bake the cake. The cooking time and temperature for the Viva is 30 minutes at 160 degrees; for the Avance XL, 50 minutes at 160 degrees.

4. Allow the cake to cool in the tin and sprinkle with powdered sugar.

APRICOT AND BLACKBERRY CRUMBLE

Serves: 4

Cook Time: 20 minutes

INGREDIENTS

- 250 g fresh apricots
- 75 g sugar
- 100 g fresh blackberries
- 1 tablespoon lemon juice
- 100 g flour
- 50 g cold butter, in cubes
- Shallow, round cake tin, 16 cm diameter

DIRECTIONS

1. Preheat the airfryer to 200°C.
2. Halve the apricots and remove the stones. Cut the apricots into cubes and mix them in a bowl with the lemon juice and 25 g sugar.
3. Grease the cake tin and spread the fruit mix over the tin.
4. In a bowl, mix the flour with a pinch of salt, the remainder of the sugar, the butter, and 1 tablespoon cold water until it is more or less consistent and then turn it into a crumbly mixture using your fingertips.
5. Distribute the crumbly mixture evenly over the fruit and press the top layer lightly.

6. Put the bowl in the basket and slide the basket into the airfryer. Set the timer to 20 minutes and bake the crumble until golden brown and done.

7. Serve the crumble hot, lukewarm, or cold with ice cream, whipped cream, or vanilla sauce.

APPLES STUFFED WITH ALMONDS

Serves: 4

Cook Time: 10 minutes

INGREDIENTS

- 4 small, firm apples
- 40 g blanched almonds
- 25 g (white) raisins
- 2 tablespoons sugar
- Vanilla sauce (see tip) or whipped cream
- Parchment paper

DIRECTIONS

1. Wash the apples and remove the cores.
2. Grind the almonds in the food processor and add the raisins, sugar, and calvados. Turn the mixture another 30 seconds in the food processor.
3. Preheat the airfryer to 180°C. Line the bottom of the basket with baking parchment, leave 1 cm of the edge open.
4. Fill the apples with the raisin mixture and put them side by side in the basket.
5. Slide the basket into the airfryer and set the timer to 10 minutes. Bake the apples until brown and done.
6. Serve the apples on plates and spoon the vanilla sauce or ice cream next to the apples.

BLUEBERRY MUFFINS

Serves: 4

Cook Time: 10 minutes

INGREDIENTS

- 175 g sugar
- 250 g low fat yogurt
- 280 g flour
- 150 g blueberries
- 1 egg
- 1 vanilla pod
- 3 teaspoons baking powder
- 1 teaspoon powdered sugar

DIRECTIONS

1. Heat the Airfryer to 160 degrees. Mix the sugar with the egg, yogurt and the seeds from one vanilla pod in the food processor. To do this, use the flat beater and turn the food processor to setting 4. Mix for 5 minutes.

2. Add in the baking powder and turn to setting number 2, then carefully add the blueberries.

3. Fill 12 muffin cases two thirds full and bake the muffins in batches of six or nine, depending on the Airfryer model, for 15 minutes at 160 degrees. Let the muffins cool then dust with powdered sugar. A real treat!

PEAR PARCEL

Serves: 4

Cook Time: 10 minutes

INGREDIENTS

- 4 sheets puff pastry
- 500 ml vanilla custard
- 2 small pears
- 1 egg, lightly beaten
- 2 tablespoons sugar
- Pinch of cinnamon
- Whipped cream
- Chocolate decoration

DIRECTIONS

1. Peel the pears and cut them in half. Remove the pips with a spoon and cut small indentations in the pears.
2. Place a small spoonful of vanilla custard in the middle of the pastry slices and place the pear on top.
3. Coat the slices with a lightly beaten egg and sprinkle with the sugar/cinnamon mixture. Heat the Airfryer to 165 degrees and bake the small individual parcels for 15 minutes.
4. Garnish the pear parcels with chocolate and whipped cream and serve with vanilla custard.

FRUIT CRUMBLE MUG CAKES

Serves: 4

Cook Time: 10 minutes

INGREDIENTS

- Philips Airfryer
- 110 g Plain Flour
- 50 g Butter
- 30 g Caster Sugar
- 30 g Gluten Free Oats
- 25 g Brown Sugar
- 4 Plums
- 1 Small Apple
- 1 Small Pear
- 1 Small Peach
- Handful Blueberries
- 1 Tbsp Honey

DIRECTIONS

1. Preheat the Air Fryer to 160c.
2. Using the corer remove the cores and the stones from the fruit and dice into very small square pieces.

3. Place the fruit in the bottom of the mugs spreading them out between the four mugs. Sprinkle with brown sugar and honey until all the fruit is well covered. Put to one side.

4. Place the flour, butter and caster sugar into a mixing bowl and rub the fat into the flour. When it resembles fine breadcrumbs you can then add the oats. Mix well.

5. Cover the tops of the mugs with a layer of your crumble.

6. Place in the Air Fryer for 10 minutes at 160c. Then after 10 minutes cook for a further 5 minutes at 200c so that you can get a lovely crunch to the top of your crumble.

AIRFRYER CHOCOLATE MUG CAKE

Serves: 4

Cook Time: 10 minutes

INGREDIENTS

- Philips Airfryer
- ¼ Cup Self Raising Flour
- 5 Tbsp Caster Sugar
- 1 Tbsp Cocoa Powder
- 3 Tbsp Whole Milk
- 3 Tsp Coconut Oil

DIRECTIONS

1. Mix all the ingredients together in the mug. But make sure they are mixed well otherwise you will end up with a cake with hardly any cocoa one time and then loads the next!

2. Place the mug in the Airfryer and cook for 10 minutes at 200c. Rinse and repeat for the other mugs until everyone has had their chocolate hit!

3. Serve!

BRITISH LEMON TARTS

Serves: 4

Cook Time: 10 minutes

INGREDIENTS

- 100 g Butter
- 225 g Plain Flour
- 30 g Caster Sugar
- 1 Large Lemon zest and juice
- 4 Tsp Lemon Curd
- Pinch Nutmeg

DIRECTIONS

1. In a large mixing bowl make your shortcrust pastry. Mix together the butter, flour and sugar using the rubbing in method. When it resembles fine breadcrumbs add the lemon rind and juice, nutmeg, then mix again. Add water a little at the time using the water to combine the ingredients until you have lovely soft dough.

2. Roll out your pastry with a little flour.

3. Using small ramekins or little pastry cases rub a little flour around them to stop them sticking and then add your pastry. Please make sure your pastry is nice and thin otherwise when cooked it will end up way too thick.

4. Add ½ teaspoon into each of your mini tart containers and then cook your lemon tarts for 15 minutes on 180c.

5. Leave to cool for a couple of minutes and then serve.

WHITE CHOCOLATE CHIP COOKIES

Serves: 4

Cook Time: 10 minutes

INGREDIENTS

- 175 g Self Raising Flour
- 100 g Butter
- 75 g Brown Sugar
- 60 g White Chocolate
- 30 ml Honey
- 30 ml Whole Milk

DIRECTIONS

- Beat the butter until it is lovely and soft. Add the sugar and beat it into the butter until you have a light and fluffy mixture.
1. Stir in the honey, flour, white chocolate and milk.
2. Mix well.
3. Make the mixture into cookie shapes and place them in the Airfryer.
4. Cook for 18 minutes at 180c or until cooked in the centre.

PINEAPPLE CAKE

Serves: 4

Cook Time: 40 minutes

INGREDIENTS

- 225 g Self Raising Flour
- 100 g Butter
- 100 g Caster Sugar
- 200 g Pineapple chopped into chunks
- 100 ml Pineapple Juice
- 50 g Dark Chocolate grated
- 1 Medium Eggs
- 2 Tbsp Whole Milk

DIRECTIONS

1. Preheat the Airfryer to 200c and grease a cake tin.
2. In a bowl mix the butter into the flour. Rub it in until the mixture resembles breadcrumbs.
3. Stir in the sugar, add the pineapple chunks and juice and add the dark chocolate. Put to one side.
4. Beat the egg and milk together in a jug.
5. Mix the liquid to the breadcrumbs mixture until you have a soft cake mixture.

6. Cook in the Airfryer for 40 minutes on a 200c heat.
7. Rest for 10 minutes and then serve.

BANANA BREAD

Serves: 4

Cook Time: 20 minutes

INGREDIENTS

- 225 g Self Raising Flour
- ¼ Tsp Bicarbonate Of Soda
- 75 g Butter
- 175 g Caster Sugar
- 2 Medium Eggs
- 450 g Bananas weight with peeling
- 100 g Chopped Walnuts

DIRECTIONS

1. Preheat the airfryer to 180c.
2. Grease a tin that will slot into your airfryer.
3. Mix together the bicarbonate of soda with the flour.
4. In a separate bowl cream the butter and sugar until pale and fluffy, then add the eggs a little at a time with a little flour with each.
5. Stir in the remaining flour and walnuts.
6. Peel the bananas and mash them up and also add them to your mixture.
7. Place the banana bread mix into the tin and cook for 10 minutes on 180c, then 15 for 170c.
8. Serve!

AIRFRYER DOUGHNUTS

Serves: 4

Cook Time: 15 minutes

INGREDIENTS

- Doughnuts
- 225 g Self Raising Flour
- 50 g Caster Sugar
- 50 g Brown Sugar
- 118 ml Whole Milk
- 1 Tsp Baking Powder
- 2.5 Tbsp Butter
- 1 Large Egg
- Strawberry Icing
- 50 g Butter
- 100 g Icing Sugar
- ½ Tsp Pink Food Colouring
- 1 Tbsp Whipped Cream
- ¼ Cup Fresh Strawberries blended

DIRECTIONS

1. Preheat the airfryer to 180c.
2. In a medium sized mixing bowl whisk together your butter, self raising flour, caster sugar and the brown sugar.

3. In another bowl mix together your milk, butter and egg.

4. Gently mix in the second bowl into the first and make sure you don't over mix as you just want the ingredients to be combined.

5. Roll the dough out until ¾ inch thickness.

6. Using a cutter remove the centre from the doughnut shapes so that they look like a pre-cooked doughnut.

7. Grease a baking sheet inside the airfryer and add your doughnuts. Cook for 15 minutes at 180c or until they spring back when lightly pressed.

8. Allow to cool for 5 minutes while you make your icing. Cream the butter and gradually add the icing sugar until you have a creamy mixture. Add the food colouring, whipped cream and blended strawberries and mix well.

9. When the doughnuts have cooled place the icing over the top.

10. Serve!

AIRFRYER CHOCOLATE ECLAIRS

Serves: 4

Cook Time: 20 minutes

INGREDIENTS

- Éclair Dough:
- 50 g Butter
- 100 g Plain Flour
- 3 Medium Eggs
- 150 ml Water
- Cream Filling:
- 1 Tsp Vanilla Essence
- 1 Tsp Icing Sugar
- 150 ml Whipped Cream
- Chocolate Topping:
- 50 g Milk Chocolate chopped into chunks
- 1 Tbsp Whipped Cream
- 25 g Butter

DIRECTIONS

1. Preheat the airfryer to 180c.
2. While it is heating up, Place fat in the water and melt over a medium heat in a large pan and then bring to the boil.
3. Remove it from the heat and stir in the flour.

4. Return the pan to the heat and stir into it forms a medium ball in the middle of the pan.

5. Transfer the dough to a cold plate so that it can cool. Once it is cool beat in the eggs until you have a smooth mixture.

6. Then make into éclair shapes and place in the Airfryer. Cook for 10 minutes on 180 and a further 8 minutes on 160.

7. While the dough is cooking make your cream filling – mix with a whisk the vanilla essence, whipped cream and icing sugar until nice and thick.

8. Leave the eclairs to cool and while they are cooling make your chocolate topping – Place the milk chocolate, whipped cream and butter into a glass bowl. Place it over a pan of hot water and mix well until you have melted chocolate.

9. Cover the tops of the eclairs with melted chocolate and then serve!

AIRFRYER CHOCOLATE BROWNIES

Serves: 4

Cook Time: 20 minutes

INGREDIENTS

- 125 g Caster Sugar
- 2 Tbsp Water
- 142 ml Milk
- 125 g Butter
- 50 g Chocolate
- 175 g Brown Sugar
- 2 Medium Eggs beaten
- 100 g Self Raising Flour
- 2 Tsp Vanilla Essence

DIRECTIONS

1. Preheat your airfryer to 180c.
2. Start by preparing the chocolate brownies – Melt 100g of the butter and chocolate over a medium heat in a bowl above a pan. Stir in the brown sugar, add the medium eggs and then add the vanilla essence. Add the self raising flour and mix well.
3. Pour the mixture into a greased dish that is of an appropriate size for your airfryer.
4. Cook in your airfryer for 15 minutes on a 180c.

5. While the brownies are cooking it is time to make the caramel sauce – Mix the caster sugar and the water in a pan on a medium heat until the sugar is melted. Then turn it up and cook for a further three minutes until it has turned a light brown colour. Take off the heat and then after 2 minutes add your butter and keep stirring until it is all melted. Then slowly add the milk.

6. Set the caramel sauce to one side for it to cool.

7. When the brownies are ready chop them into squares and place them on a plate with some sliced banana and cover with some caramel sauce.

8. Serve!

MINI APPLE PIES

Serves: 4

Cook Time: 20 minutes

INGREDIENTS

- 75 g Plain Flour
- 33 g Butter
- 15 g Caster Sugar
- Water
- 2 Medium Red Apples
- Pinch Cinnamon
- Pinch Caster Sugar

DIRECTIONS

1. Preheat your airfryer to 180c.
2. Start by making your pastry – place the plain flour and butter in a mixing bowl and rub the fat into the flour. Add the sugar and mix well. Add the water until the ingredients are moist enough to combine into a nice dough. Knead the dough well until it has a smooth texture.
3. Cover your pastry tins with butter to stop it sticking and then roll out the pastry and fill your pastry tins.
4. Peel and dice your apples and place in the tins. Sprinkle them with sugar and cinnamon.
5. Add an extra pastry layer to the top and make some fork markings so that they can breathe.
6. Cook in the airfryer for 18 minutes.

HEART SHAPED COOKIES

Serves: 4

Cook Time: 20 minutes

INGREDIENTS

- Heart Shaped Cutter
- 250 g Plain Flour
- 75 g Caster Sugar
- 175 g Butter
- 1 Tsp Vanilla Essence
- Chocolate Buttons

DIRECTIONS

1. Preheat the air fryer to 180c.
2. In a mixing bowl place all your ingredients apart from your chocolate and rub the fat into the other ingredients.
3. It will soon rub into each other to create a nice soft dough.
4. When it is a big dough ball roll it out and cut it into heart shapes with your cutter.
5. Place it into the air fryer on top of a baking sheet with a little gap in between each one. Cook for 10 minutes on 180c.
6. Open the air fryer and place the chocolate buttons into the top of the half baked dough.
7. Cook for a further 10 minutes on 160c and serve with hot chocolate and marshmallows.

CHOCOLATE CHRISTMAS BISCUITS

Serves: 4

Cook Time: 15 minutes

INGREDIENTS

- 225 g Self Raising Flour
- 100 g Caster Sugar
- 100 g Butter
- 1 Large Orange juice and rind
- 1 Large Egg beaten
- 2 Tbsp Cocoa Powder
- 2 Tsp Vanilla Essence
- 8 Dark Chocolate

DIRECTIONS

1. Preheat your air fryer to 180c.
2. In a mixing bowl add your butter and flour and rub the fat into the flour until your ingredients resemble breadcrumbs.
3. Add your sugar, vanilla, orange and cocoa powder and mix well.
4. Add your egg and mix well until your mixture resembles a dough that is a little wet.
5. Place some flour onto your hands so that the mixture doesn't stick to you and make balls out of your dough into 8 equal sized portions.

6. Flatten your balls of dough and place a square of dark chocolate inside each piece and then wrap the dough around it so that you can't see the chocolate.

7. Place all 8 pieces into the air fryer on 180c for 15 minutes.

8. Serve.

AIRFRYER OATY SANDWICH BISCUITS

Serves: 4

Cook Time: 10 minutes

INGREDIENTS

- 150 g Plain Flour
- 100 g Butter
- 75 g White Sugar
- ½ Small Egg beaten
- ¼ Cup Desiccated Coconut
- ½ Cup Gluten Free Oats
- 20 g White Chocolate
- 1 Tsp Vanilla Essence
- For the filling:
- 100 g Icing Sugar
- 50 g Butter
- ½ Small Lemon juice only
- 1 Tsp Vanilla Essence

DIRECTIONS

1. Cream the butter and the sugar together until it is light and fluffy. Add the egg, chocolate, coconut and vanilla essence. Add the flour and mix well.

2. Make into medium sized biscuit shapes and then roll in the oats.

3. Place in the Airfryer for 18 minutes on 180c.

4. While they are cooling make your filling. Cream the icing sugar and the butter until you have a lovely creamy mixture. Add the lemon juice and the vanilla, mix again and then put to one side.

5. When the biscuits are cool add the filling and press together so that they resemble a nice sandwich.

AIRFRYER LEMON BISCUITS

Serves: 4

Cook Time: 10 minutes

INGREDIENTS

- 100 g Butter
- 100 g Caster Sugar
- 225 g Self Raising Flour
- 1 Small Lemon rind and juice
- 1 Small Egg
- 1 Tsp Vanilla Essence

DIRECTIONS

1. Preheat the airfryer to 180c.
2. Mix flour and sugar in a bowl. Add the butter and rub it in until your mix resembles breadcrumbs. Shake your bowl regularly so that the fat bits come to the top and so that you know what you have left to rub in.
3. Add the lemon rind and juice along with the egg.
4. Combine and knead until you have lovely soft dough.
5. Roll out and cut into medium sized biscuits.
6. Place the biscuits into the airfryer on a baking sheet and cook for five minutes at 180c.
7. Place on a cooling tray and sprinkle with icing sugar.

HALF DIPPED CHOCOLATE BISCUITS

Serves: 4

Cook Time: 20 minutes

INGREDIENTS

- 225 g Self Raising Flour
- 100 g White Sugar
- 100 g Butter
- 50 g Milk Chocolate
- 1 Small Egg beaten
- 1 Tsp Vanilla Essence

DIRECTIONS

1. In a mixing bowl add the flour, sugar and butter. Rub the butter into the flour until your mixture resembles breadcrumbs.

2. Add the vanilla essence and the egg (a little at a time) until you are able to create a dough from your mixture.

3. Make into walnut sized balls and place in the Airfryer for 15 minutes at 180c.

4. While the biscuits are cooling melt the milk chocolate in the Airfryer. I find 4 minutes at 180c is enough and keep stirring it until you have a lovely chocolate liquid.

5. When the biscuits are cool dip one side in the chocolate and place them in the fridge for about an hour so that they can set.

VEGAN DESSERTS

COFFEE DOUGHNUT HOLES

Serves: 4

Cook Time: 10 minutes

INGREDIENTS

- 1 cup white all purpose flour
- ¼ cup organic sugar
- 1 teaspoon baking powder
- ½ teaspoon salt
- 2 tablespoons aquafaba (I have used white bean and chickpea to make these, and both worked great!)
- 1 tablespoon neutral oil, like sunflower
- ¼ cup coffee
- 1 teaspoon coffee extract
- 1 batch Coffee Maple Cream

INSTRUCTIONS

1. In a large bowl, combine the flour, sugar, baking powder and salt. Mix well.

2. Add the aquafaba, oil, coffee, and coffee extract. Mix well. I had the best results when I mixed with a fork, then got in with my hands and kneaded the dough together for a few seconds when it got too stiff to beat with a fork. When you're done, you should have a ball of slightly sticky dough.

3. Stick the bowl of dough into the refrigerator for at least an hour. You can even make the dough the night before. If you do this, store in an airtight container.

4. This is a good time to make that Coffee Maple Cream. See the recipe below this one.

5. Air Fryer Directions: Cut a piece of parchment paper so it covers some of the bottom of your air fryer but doesn't cover it completely. I use a square cut about 1" smaller than the bottom, leaving plenty of room for air to circulate. Remove the dough from the fridge, and give it a quick knead. Divide into 12 pieces, forming the pieces into balls. Optional: You can roll the doughnut holes in sugar before air frying, if you want a crunchier result. Arrange into a single layer on the parchment paper, leaving at least 1" of room around each ball. I air fried mine in 2 batches of 6 doughnut holes each. Air fry at 370F for 6 minutes.

VEGAN AIR FRYER BLUEBERRY APPLE CRUMBLE

Serves: 4

Cook Time: 20 minutes

INGREDIENTS

- 1 medium apple, finely diced
- ½ cup frozen blueberries, strawberries, or peaches
- ¼ cup plus 1 tablespoon brown rice flour
- 2 tablespoons sugar
- ½ teaspoon ground cinnamon
- 2 tablespoons nondairy butter

INSTRUCTIONS

1. Preheat the air fryer to 350°F for 5 minutes. Combine the apple and frozen blueberries in an air fryer–safe baking pan or ramekin.

2. In a small bowl, combine the flour, sugar, cinnamon, and butter. Spoon the flour mixture over the fruit. Sprinkle a little extra flour over everything to cover any exposed fruit. Cook at 350°F for 15 minutes.

CHILI-GINGER TAHINI DRESSING

Serves: 4

Cook Time: 0 minutes

INGREDIENTS

- 2 cubes Dorot Crushed Garlic or 2 cloves minced garlic
- 2-3 teaspoons chili sauce I like Sriracha sauce or Sambal Oelek in this recipe., depending on how spicy you want it
- 2-3 cubes Dorot Crushed Ginger or 2-3 teaspoons minced ginger, depending on how spicy you want it
- ¾ cups tahini
- ¾ cup water
- 1 teaspoon agave nectar
- 1 teaspoon soy sauce or 1 tablespoon light soy sauce
- juice of 1 fresh lime

INSTRUCTIONS

1. Combine all of your ingredients in your blender, and puree until smooth.
2. If needed, add more water by the tablespoon to reach your desired thickness.

SALTY PISTACHIO BROWNIES

Serves: 4

Cook Time: 20 minutes

INGREDIENTS

- ¼ cup (60ml) nondairy milk
- ¼ cup (60ml) aquafaba
- ½ teaspoon vanilla extract
- ½ cup (48g) whole wheat pastry flour (*use gluten-free baking blend)
- ½ cup (99g) vegan sugar (or sweetener of choice, to taste)
- ¼ cup (21g) cocoa powder
- 1 tablespoon (6g) ground flax seeds
- ¼ teaspoon salt
- mix ins: ¼ cup of any one or a combination of the following: chopped walnuts, hazelnuts, pecans, mini vegan chocolate chips, shredded coconut

INSTRUCTIONS

1. Mix the dry ingredients together in one bowl.
2. Then mix the wet ingredients in a large measuring cup. Add the wet to the dry and mix well.
3. Add in the mix-in(s) of your choice and mix again.
4. Preheat your air fryer to 350 °F (or as close as your air fryer gets).

5. Either spray some oil on a 5-inch cake or pie round pan (or a loaf pan that fits in your air fryer), or line it with parchment paper to keep it completely oil-free.

6. Place the pan in the fryer basket. Cook for 20 minutes. If the middle is not well set or a knife doesn't come out clean when stuck in the middle cook for 5 minutes more and repeat as needed. The time may vary depending on the size pan and your particular air fryer.

VEGAN PUMPKIN BREAD PUDDING

Serves: 4

Cook Time: 60 minutes

INGREDIENTS

- 1 16 ounce loaf French bread
- ½ cup raisins
- 1 ½ cup soymilk or other non-dairy milk vanilla or plain
- 1 cup pumpkin canned or cooked and pureed
- ¼ cup maple syrup
- ¼ cup dark brown sugar
- 1 tablespoon Ener-G Egg Replacer may substitute 2 ½ tsp. starch (tapioca, potato, or corn starch) plus ½ tsp. baking powder
- 2 teaspoons vanilla extract
- 1 ½ teaspoon cinnamon
- ½ teaspoon ginger powder
- ½ teaspoon nutmeg
- ¼ teaspoon allspice
- 1/8 teaspoon ground cloves
- ¼ teaspoon salt optional
- Sauce
- ½ cup apple cider or juice
- ¼ cup maple syrup

- 1 teaspoon cornstarch mixed with 1 tablespoon apple juice
- 1 ½ tablespoons brandy, rum, or bourbon add to taste up to ¼ cup
- ¼ cup chopped pecans or walnuts optional

INSTRUCTIONS

1. Cut or tear the bread into bite-sized pieces. If the bread seems moist or dense, spread it out on a cookie sheet and toast it for a few minutes in the oven. Place it in a large bowl and add the raisins.

2. Put the non-dairy milk into the blender along with the pumpkin, maple syrup, sugar, Ener-G, vanilla, spices, and salt. Blend until smooth. Pour it over the bread, using a silicone spatula to get out every drop. Stir well to completely coat all of the bread. Set aside to soak for a few minutes while you ready the pan and preheat the oven.

3. Preheat oven to 350F. Line an 8x8-inch baking dish with parchment paper or oil lightly. Pour the bread pudding into the pan in an even layer. Bake for about 45 minutes or until top is set and beginning to brown. Remove from oven and allow to cool for at least 15 minutes.

4. While the pudding is cooling make the sauce. Place the apple cider and maple syrup in a small saucepan over medium heat, and bring to a simmer, stirring often, until reduced to about half.

5. Carefully add the cornstarch mixture, bring to a boil, and cook for another couple of minutes, stirring constantly, until mixture is no longer cloudy and thickens slightly. Remove from heat and add the brandy or other spirits a little at a time, to taste. Stir in the nuts. Poke a few holes in the top of the bread pudding with a toothpick, and pour the sauce over the top, distributing nuts evenly. Cut into squares and serve warm.

VEGAN IRISH CREAM CHEESECAKE

Serves: 4

Cook Time: 55 minutes

INGREDIENTS

- 12.3 ounces extra firm silken tofu (Mori-nu brand)
- 8 ounces Tofutti Better Than Cream Cheese (non-hydrogenated formula)
- ¾ cup sugar
- ½ cup Bailey's Almande
- 2 tablespoons Almond Milk (or additional Almande)
- 2 tablespoons lemon or lime juice
- ½ teaspoon vanilla extract
- ½ teaspoon freshly ground nutmeg
- 3 tablespoons cornstarch
- 1 prepared pie crust
- grated chocolate optional

INSTRUCTIONS

1. Preheat the oven to 350 F. Drain the tofu and put it and all ingredients except pie crust and chocolate into your food processor. Blend until completely smooth. Pour into a prepared pie crust and bake in the middle of the oven for about 55 minutes (do not allow to brown). Filling will be slightly jiggly, not completely set until chilled.

2. Remove from oven and allow to cool. Refrigerate until completely chilled (the longer, the better). Serve sprinkled with grated chocolate if desired.

CRANBERRY-CARROT CAKE

Serves: 4

Cook Time: 40 minutes

INGREDIENTS

- 8-10 ounces fresh cranberries
- ⅓ cup natural granulated sugar
- 1 ¾ cups whole wheat pastry flour (or white whole wheat flour)
- 2 tablespoons ground flaxseeds
- 1 teaspoon baking powder
- ½ teaspoon baking soda
- ½ teaspoon ground ginger
- ½ teaspoon cinnamon
- ½ cup applesauce
- ⅓ cup maple syrup
- 2 tablespoons aquafaba (liquid from canned or cooked chickpeas) or plant milk of choice
- 1 teaspoon vanilla extract
- 1 cup grated carrot
- Maple-Cream Cheese frosting optional (see recipe in Notes)
- ⅓ cup finely chopped walnuts optional
- confectioners sugar optional

INSTRUCTIONS

1. Place the cranberries in a food processor fitted with the blade and pulse on and off until evenly and finely chopped. Transfer to a bowl. Add the sugar, stir well, and set aside.

2. Preheat oven to 350F.

3. In a large mixing bowl, combine the flour, flaxseeds, baking powder, baking soda, ginger, and cinnamon. Stir to combine thoroughly.

4. Make a well in the center and add the applesauce, syrup, aquafaba/plant milk, and vanilla. Stir until the wet and dry ingredients are completely combined, but don't over mix.

5. Stir the cranberries and carrots into the batter. Pour into a 9-inch round silicone cake pan. or lightly oiled springform pan (see headnote). Bake for 35 to 40 minutes, or until a knife inserted into the center comes out clean.

6. If using the walnuts, toast them in a small dry skillet over medium heat until they brown lightly.

7. Once the cake has cooled to room temperature, release from the pan if you've used a springform or other easy-to-release pan and spread the frosting over the top evenly, allowing it to drip over the sides. Otherwise, leave the cake in the pan and simply frost the top.

8. (If you don't wish to use the frosting, you can sprinkle the top with confectioners sugar or just serve it plain.)

9. Sprinkle evenly with the optional walnuts, then cut into wedges to serve.

VEGAN GLUTEN-FREE PEACH COBBLER

Serves: 4

Cook Time: 40 minutes

INGREDIENTS

- Peaches
- 2 pounds peaches (about 5 large)
- 1 teaspoon lemon juice
- 2 tablespoons sugar
- ¼ teaspoon cinnamon optional
- Dry
- 1 cup gluten-free baking flour blend
- ½ cup sugar
- 2 tablespoons tapioca starch (also called tapioca flour)
- 1 tablespoon baking powder
- Pinch salt
- Wet
- ¾ cup soy milk or other non-dairy milk
- ½ teaspoon vanilla extract

INSTRUCTIONS

1. Bring several inches of water to boil in a large saucepan. Use a slotted spoon to lower each peach into the boiling water for about 20 seconds. Place on a cutting board or plate and set aside to cool. (This makes the

peaches easy to peel.)

2. When the peaches are cool enough, peel them by piercing the skin with a knife and pulling it off. Slice the peaches into a large bowl. Add the lemon juice, 2 tablespoons sugar, and cinnamon, if desired.

3. Preheat oven to 375F. Arrange the peaches in a deep 9-inch pie pan.

4. Mix the dry ingredients together. Add the wet ingredients, and stir just enough to eliminate large lumps. Pour over the peaches.

5. Bake for 35-45 minutes, covering loosely with aluminum foil if the top begins to get too brown. It's done with you can stick a toothpick in the middle and not have batter stuck to it.

6. Allow to cool for a few minutes before serving.

PEAR SPICE UPSIDE-DOWN CAKE

Serves: 4

Cook Time: 40 minutes

INGREDIENTS

- Dry:
- 1 ½ cups white whole wheat flour or whole wheat pastry flour
- 1 tablespoon cornstarch
- 1 ½ teaspoons baking soda
- ½ teaspoon cinnamon
- ½ teaspoon ground ginger
- ½ teaspoon freshly ground nutmeg
- ¼ teaspoon salt
- 1/8 teaspoon ground cloves
- Pears:
- 3 large pears I used Bosc
- 2 tablespoons water
- applesauce if necessary
- Liquid:
- ¾ cup maple syrup or combination of agave and maple syrup divided
- 1 tablespoon lemon juice
- 1 teaspoon vanilla extract

INSTRUCTIONS

1. Preheat oven to 350. Line the bottom of a 9-inch round non-stick baking pan with parchment paper cut to fit.

2. In a medium mixing bowl, combine the dry ingredients and stir well. Set aside.

3. Peel the pears. Cut one of them into thin slices about ¼-inch thick (avoiding the core). Chop the other two into large chunks (again, no core).

4. Arrange the sliced pear in the prepared pan in any design you wish. Don't worry about using all the slices--just as many as will fit or fit your idea of the design. Pour ¼ cup of the maple syrup over the pears. Reserve the rest.

5. Put the extra slices and the pear chunks into the blender with 2 tablespoons water. Blend, stopping if necessary to push down any stray pears, until it's about the consistency of applesauce.

6. Measure out 1 2/3 cups of the pear sauce. Reserve any extra for another use (it's good on a fruit salad or in a smoothie). If there's not enough, add applesauce until you have 1 2/3 cups.

7. Make a well in the dry ingredients and pour in the 1 2/3 cups of pear sauce. Add the remaining ½ cup of maple syrup and the other liquid ingredients. Stir until combined but don't over-stir. Carefully spoon the batter over the pears so that you don't move them and change the design.

8. Bake for 35-45 minutes, testing by inserting a toothpick in the middle. It's ready when the toothpick comes out clean.

9. Run a knife around the edge of the pan to loosen any stuck on parts of the cake. Place a serving dish over it and invert. Tap lightly to dislodge the cake from the pan. Loosen all the edges of the parchment paper and then slowly peel it back, using a knife or your fingers to push back into place any pieces of pear that want to stick to it. If there is glaze

left on the paper, scrape it off with a knife and smooth it onto the cake.

10. Peeling back the parchment
11. Allow to cool. Cut into 8 slices and enjoy!

BANANA BREAD PUDDING

Serves: 4

Cook Time: 50 minutes

INGREDIENTS

- 1 16-ounce loaf French bread
- ½ cup raisins
- 1 ½ cup unsweetened almond milk vanilla or plain (or other non-dairy milk)
- 1 cup mashed overripe bananas
- ¼ cup maple syrup
- ¼ cup dark brown sugar
- 2 teaspoons cornstarch or potato starch
- 2 teaspoons vanilla extract
- 1 ½ teaspoon cinnamon
- ½ teaspoon baking powder
- ½ teaspoon nutmeg
- ¼ teaspoon allspice
- SAUCE
- ½ cup apple cider or apple juice
- ¼ cup maple syrup
- 1 teaspoon cornstarch mixed with 1 tablespoon apple juice
- 1 ½ - 2 tablespoons brandy, rum, or bourbon (see Notes below)
- ¼ cup chopped pecans or walnuts optional

INSTRUCTIONS

1. Cut or tear the bread into bite-sized pieces. If the bread seems moist or dense, spread it out on a cookie sheet and toast it for a few minutes in the oven. Place it in a large bowl and add the raisins.

2. Put the non-dairy milk into the blender along with the banana, maple syrup, sugar, cornstarch, vanilla, baking powder, and spices. Blend until smooth. Pour it over the bread, using a silicone spatula to get out every drop. Stir well to completely coat all of the bread. Set aside to soak for a few minutes while you ready the pan and preheat the oven.

3. Preheat oven to 350F. Line an 8×8-inch baking dish with parchment paper or oil lightly. Pour the bread pudding into the pan in an even layer. Bake for about 45 minutes or until top is set and beginning to brown. Remove from oven and allow to cool for at least 15 minutes.

4. While the pudding is cooling, make the sauce. Place the apple cider and maple syrup in a small saucepan over medium heat, and bring to a simmer, stirring often, until reduced to about half. Carefully add the cornstarch mixture and stirring constantly, bring to a boil and cook for another couple of minutes, until mixture is no longer cloudy. Remove from heat and add the brandy or other spirits a little at a time, to taste. Stir in the nuts. Poke a few holes in the top of the bread pudding with a toothpick, and pour the sauce over the top, distributing nuts evenly. Cut into squares and serve warm.

DATE-SWEETENED ZUCCHINI BROWNIES WITH CHOCOLATE-PEANUT BUTTER FROSTING

Serves: 4

Cook Time: 20 minutes

INGREDIENTS

- ½ cup pitted and chopped medjool dates
- ¾ cup hot water
- ⅓ cup applesauce
- 1 teaspoon vanilla extract
- 1 cup white whole wheat or whole wheat pastry flour
- ⅓ cup cocoa powder
- ¼ cup vegan sugar, xylitol, stevia baking blend, or sweetener of choice (see note)
- ¾ teaspoon baking soda
- ¼ teaspoon salt
- 1 cup finely shredded zucchini (about ½ medium zucchini shredded in food processor)
- ¼ cup walnut pieces optional
- OPTIONAL FROSTING:
- ½ cup vegan chocolate chips
- 3 tablespoons almond milk or other non-dairy milk
- 1 tablespoon natural peanut butter or other nut butter

INSTRUCTIONS

1. Place the dates in a small bowl and pour the hot water over them. Allow to soak until the dates are soft, about ½ hour.

2. Preheat oven to 350 F. Prepare an 8×8-inch baking dish by lining it with parchment paper or oiling lightly.

3. Put the dates and the soaking water in the blender with the applesauce and vanilla. Blend at high speed until completely smooth. Set aside.

4. Combine the flour, cocoa, sugar or substitute, baking soda, and salt. Stir in the zucchini and walnuts, if using. Add the blended date mixture and stir until all the flour is moistened. The batter will be thick. Spoon it into the prepared pan and smooth over the top.

5. Bake for about 25 minutes, or until brownies are no longer liquid in the middle and edges are firm but not drying out. Allow to cool.

6. You can eat them plain or add the Chocolate-Peanut Butter Frosting:

7. Combine the chocolate chips, non-dairy milk, and nut butter in a small microwaveable bowl or the top of a double boiler. If microwaving, cook on high for 30 seconds, stir, and repeat microwaving and stirring for 10-second intervals, until frosting is smooth. In double boiler, cook and stir until chocolate is melted and mixture is smooth. Frost brownies immediately. Allow to stand about 20 minutes to firm up. Enjoy!

APPLE PIE OATMEAL COOKIES

Serves: 4

Cook Time: 10 minutes

INGREDIENTS

- 2 teaspoons chia seeds or ground flax seeds
- 4 tablespoons warm water
- 2 cup regular or quick oats (use certified gluten-free if necessary)
- ¼ cup raisins
- 1 ½ teaspoon pumpkin pie spice see Notes
- ½ teaspoon baking soda
- ½ teaspoon salt optional
- 1 large apple cored and chopped
- 2 ounces pitted and chopped dates (about 4 medjool dates or ¼ cup packed chopped dates)
- 1/8 cup water
- 1 teaspoon apple cider vinegar

INSTRUCTIONS

1. Preheat the oven to 375.
2. In a small bowl, combine the chia seeds (or ground flaxseed) with the warm water and set aside until thickened.
3. In a dry blender or food processor, grind one cup of the oats. Pour it into a mixing bowl and add the unground oats, pumpkin pie spice, baking soda, and salt. Stir in the raisins.

4. Place the apple, dates, 1/8 cup water, and apple cider vinegar in the blender. Blend until it's about the consistency of apple sauce. Pour it into the oat mixture along with the chia "egg" and stir to combine.

5. Drop by rounded tablespoons onto a baking sheet lined with a silicon mat or parchment paper. Flatten each cookie slightly with a fork. Bake for about 12 minutes. Cool on a wire rack before serving.

PUMPKIN OATMEAL CAKES WITH APPLE-PECAN COMPOTE

Serves: 4

Cook Time: 30 minutes

INGREDIENTS

- 2 cups water
- ½ cup chopped dates about 3 ounces
- ¾ cups canned pumpkin
- ¾ teaspoon cinnamon
- ¼ teaspoon allspice
- ¼ teaspoon powdered ginger
- ½ teaspoon salt
- 1 tablespoon ground flaxseed
- 1 ½ cups steel-cut oats
- 1 ¼ cup plain coconut milk (the drinking kind, not canned) or other non-dairy milk
- non-stick spray

INSTRUCTIONS

1. Place the water and dates in a blender and blend until dates are finely chopped. Add the pumpkin, spices, salt, and flaxseed and blend until well-combined.

2. Heat a large saucepan and toast the oats, stirring occasionally, until fragrant, 1-2 minutes. Carefully add the pumpkin mixture, standing

back in case it spatters, and then the coconut milk. Stir well, reduce heat to low, and cook, stirring frequently, for about 30 minutes or until thick and chewy.

3. Line a 11×7-inch baking dish with parchment paper or spray with non-stick spray. Spread the oats in the dish, smoothing the top. Cool on the counter for an hour and then refrigerate until completely chilled, at least an hour. Turn out onto a cutting board and cut into 16 triangles or rectangles.

4. Spray a large non-stick frying pan with a light coating of cooking spray and heat over medium-high heat. Add half of the oatmeal cakes and cook on each side until lightly browned, 2-3 minutes per side. Remove to a warm oven and repeat with remaining cakes. Keep warm until ready to serve.

5. Place two cakes on each dessert plate. Top with warm Apple-Pecan Compote, below.

PEACH OATMEAL BARS

Serves: 4

Cook Time: 20 minutes

INGREDIENTS

- 2 cups old fashioned or rolled oats
- ¼ cup chopped dates
- 2 tablespoons chopped almonds
- 1 tablespoon chia seed or ground flax seeds
- 1 teaspoon baking powder
- 1 teaspoon cinnamon
- 1/8 teaspoon pure stevia extract powder optional
- ¾ cup plus 2 tablespoons non-dairy milk I used vanilla soymilk
- 2 peaches about 1 ¼ cups, peeled and diced
- 1 teaspoon vanilla
- ¼ teaspoon almond extract

INSTRUCTIONS

1. Preheat oven to 350F. Line a 8×8- or 9×9-inch baking pan with parchment paper (this makes sure they don't stick and makes clean-up a breeze).
2. Combine dry ingredients (oats through stevia) in a large bowl. In a medium bowl, combine remaining ingredients. Stir the wet ingredients into the dry, making sure that they are thoroughly combined. Spread into prepared pan. Bake for about 25 minutes. If you'd like a crunchier

top, put the pan under the broiler for a minute or two, watching carefully to make sure they don't burn.

3. Remove from oven and allow to cool for at least 15 minutes. Remove from pan by lifting up parchment paper. Cut into 9 squares and enjoy.

APPLESAUCE GINGER CAKE WITH MAPLE GLAZE

Serves: 4

Cook Time: 40 minutes

INGREDIENTS

- 2 cups white whole wheat flour or whole wheat pastry flour
- 1 cup sugar
- 2 tablespoons crystallized (candied) ginger , chopped small (about ¾ ounce)
- 1 tablespoon cornstarch
- 2 teaspoons baking soda
- 1 ½ teaspoon ginger powder
- ½ teaspoon salt
- ½ teaspoon cinnamon
- 1/8 teaspoon cloves
- 2 ¼ cups unsweetened applesauce
- 1 tablespoon lemon juice
- 1 teaspoon vanilla extract
- Glaze
- ¼ cup maple syrup
- 1 teaspoon cornstarch
- 1 pinch ginger powder
- Additional candied ginger for serving optional

INSTRUCTIONS

1. Preheat oven to 350 degrees. Lightly oil a bundt pan or 9×9-inch baking pan.

2. Mix the dry ingredients together; then add the applesauce, lemon juice, and vanilla extract. Stir until combined but don't over-stir. Pour into prepared pan and bake for 45-60 minutes. Test by inserting a toothpick into the center; it's done when the toothpick comes out perfectly clean.

3. Remove from oven and allow to cool for 10 minutes. Invert onto cake dish.

4. Prepare the glaze: Combine the maple syrup, 1 teaspoon cornstarch, and generous pinch of powdered ginger in a small saucepan and mix well. Bring to a boil over medium-high heat, stirring constantly. Boil for 1 minute. Remove from heat and allow to cool and thicken. (You can put the pan in a bowl of cold water to speed up cooling.) When the glaze has thickened but is still pourable, drizzle it over the cake. Serve immediately, garnished with strips of candied ginger, if desired.

www.ingramcontent.com/pod-product-compliance
Lightning Source LLC
Chambersburg PA
CBHW061149140225
21966CB00027B/281